Burial Rites for Adults
together with a
Rite for the Burial of a Child

Enriching Our Worship 3

Supplemental Liturgical Materials

prepared by
The Standing Commission on Liturgy and Music

2006

CHURCH PUBLISHING
an imprint of
Church Publishing Incorporated, New York

Church Publishing Incorporated
445 Fifth Avenue
New York, NY 10016
www.churchpublishing.org

Material from the following, as noted in the text, has been used by permission:

Celebrating Common Prayer: A version of the Daily Office SSF. © 1992 by the European Province of the Society of Saint Francis.

Common Worship: Services and Prayers for the Church of England. Church House Publishing, London. © 2000 by the Archbishops' Council.

The Book of Alternative Services of the Anglican Church of Canada. Anglican Book Centre, Toronto. © 1985 by the General Synod of the Anglican Church of Canada.

The Alternative Service Book 1980: Services Authorised for Use in the Church of England in Conjunction with the Book of Common Prayer, together with the Liturgical Psalter. Clowes, SPCK, and Cambridge University Press. © 1980 by the Central Board of Finance of the Church of England.

A New Zealand Prayer Book. William Collins Publishers Ltd. © 1989 by the Anglican Church in Aotearoa, New Zealand and Polynesia.

5 4 3 2 1

Contents

Foreword

The death of a parishioner, friend, family member, or even a stranger, is a moment of pastoral and evangelical ministry that comes with regularity in the life of a congregation. Our response to those moments comes in the central message of our faith: the new life God continues to bring out of the loss and devastation of death, most explicitly in the passion, death, and resurrection of Jesus Christ. The death of a member of the human family calls for the best of our ministry of compassion and care, and the best of our ability to proclaim that continuing good news of new life in the face of death.

This collection provides many useful pastoral and liturgical options that can expand the gracious ministry of this Church to a variety of people at what are often the most pastorally challenging moments of their lives. Included are prayers for circumstances largely unrecognized by the 1979 Book of Common Prayer—suicide, the death of a child, and death in the midst of an interfaith family. We are charged to bring good news to all people, in all circumstances, and at all times, and the prayers, psalms, readings, and hymns offered here are means to aid that work. They are only aids, however, for the greatest need of the grieving is usually incarnate reminders of the presence of God, "God with skin on," in neighbors, friends, family, fellow parishioners, and yes, even strangers, who continue to show the good news of God-with-us, who suffers with us and companions us to the grave and beyond.

The greatest opportunity for new pastoral formation and practice in this collection could be the use of vigils. It has been exceedingly rare in my experience to see a family choose anything more than a time of visitation at the funeral home. The expanded provision for vigils is a pastoral opportunity for that kind of ministry of presence which has been lost in our hurried lives. Until 100 years ago it was commonplace to keep the body at home until burial, with family and friends gathering with the bereaved to pray and remember the newly dead. Marking the hours until burial with prayer and readings is a renewed possibility of recovering that ministry of presence, as well as a claiming of sacred "time out of time." For Christians, it is also an opportunity to gather in hope and remember the promise of new life rather than staying locked at home or in a figurative upper room, consumed with fear.

This collection of rites and resources, drawn from several strands of the tradition, is a gift to our Church and its ministry of compassion. May its use speak good news to those in grief, and may those who use it be the healing presence of Jesus to the suffering.

—*The Most Reverend Katharine Jefferts Schori*
  Presiding Bishop and Primate

Preface

During the General Convention of 1976, a sub-committee of the Legislative Committee on Prayer Book and Liturgy was charged with the final editorial work on the Pastoral Offices of the *Draft Proposed Book of Common Prayer*. They were given six hours to do their work, with a 6:00 a.m. printer's deadline. Since the form for the "Celebration and Blessing of a Marriage" had attracted a significant negative response, the majority of the time available had to be spent addressing those issues. The clock ran out just as the group arrived at the Order for Burial of the Dead, Rite II. Much could have been done to perfect a modern burial office, but there was no time.

In a variety of ways since 1976, death has become something of a movable feast. By tradition, since 1789, our burial offices were designed to address situations in which death was a natural process, taking place at home or in a hospital, when the patient ceased breathing. There was one burial rite, with few options. By the last third of the twentieth century, leaving aside accidents, wars, and other tragedies in which people died suddenly and unprepared, a significant number of deaths began to occur in hospitals after heroic medical measures were withdrawn, through negotiated agreements between families and medical personnel. This new way of death was first addressed by a committee of the Diocese of Washington, D.C., and then by the Expansive Language Committee appointed by Presiding Bishop Frank Griswold in 1995, in *Enriching Our*

Worship 2 (pp. 117-123). That same volume also restored a discrete rite for the Burial of a Child, which had been omitted from the *Draft Proposed Book of Common Prayer* in 1976. (That rite is included in this volume, pp. 39-56, as an aid to the presider.)

During the same period, funeral observances also began to evolve from a single burial rite, with or without an attached Committal, to a series of observances at different times and places. Thus, Christian burial practices are gradually moving closer to the series of events provided for in modern Jewish usage. For instance, *The Authorized Daily Prayer Book*, by J.H. Hertz, provides for a House Service prior to a Funeral, a Burial Service, a Service after Burial in the House of Mourning, and a Service at the Setting of a Grave Marker. While significantly different in content, this pattern, or one very much like it, is becoming more and more frequent in Christian burial practice.

Since the approval and publication of *Enriching Our Worship 2*, the Standing Commission on Liturgy and Music has been working to address issues around funeral observance—especially provisions for expanding the ceremonies preceding the main burial rite, along with suggestions for a variety of other special circumstances. We had hoped to offer an original form for a Vigil in Spanish, but, once again, the clock ran out on us. This need must be addressed by a future commission.

One consequence of our mobile society is that people frequently die in one place and are buried, after a variety of rites, in another place. A simple acknowledgment of that fact is offered here. We also address the increasing impact of specialized cemeteries in which traditional grave-side rites are not permitted. For pastoral reasons, the Church is often asked to bury family members or friends who are members of non-Christian religions or "whose faith is known to God alone," for whom the burial rites of the Book of Common Prayer would not be appropriate. We offer an update of a model from J.B. Bernardin's *Burial Services*, with significant new material, to meet such needs. While less common in the United

States than in Europe, our country has seen an increase in burial rites in crematoriums. Provision is also offered here for those circumstances. As formal anniversary events increase, provision is also offered for these. This might include the unveiling of a grave marker, as well as anniversary commemorations in the home, or in the context of church services.

Finally, subsequent to the General Convention's approval of the *Draft Proposed Book of Common Prayer*, as amended, in 1976, other provinces of the Anglican Communion have framed very creative work in the matter of burial rites. Especially notable examples come from Anglicans in Canada, England, New Zealand, and Scotland. Some of their efforts are included here in prayers, optional additions to the lectionary, the Reception of a Body, and the Commendation. We also wish to acknowledge a debt to our ecumenical partners in the Evangelical Lutheran Church in America. Their recent work, *Renewing Worship*, provided valuable additions to our work, and a mirror in which to assess its utility.

The *Enriching Our Worship* series has tried to be faithful to the shape and direction of the Book of Common Prayer, 1979, while offering provision for language and circumstances not anticipated by that work. We hope the rites offered in this latest volume will be received as faithful to the intentions of the Book of Common Prayer and useful in helping our people to gain a more profound understanding of the Church's traditional teaching on death, in the midst of a secular society which either denies the fact of death, or treats it as an end, rather than a beginning of new life in Christ.

The Rev. Canon Gregory M. Howe,
Custodian of the Standard Book of Common Prayer
For the Standing Commission on Liturgy and Music
August 2006

Introduction

We are an Easter people. The Christian liturgy for the dead is an Easter liturgy. Because God raised Jesus from the dead, we too shall be raised. "I am Resurrection and I am life," says Christ.

Therefore, in the Church's burial service the principal theme is of joyous expectation that "neither death, nor life, nor angels, nor principalities, nor things present, nor things to come, nor powers, nor height, nor depth, nor anything else in all creation will be able to separate us from the love of God in Christ Jesus our Lord." Nonetheless, we also grieve for our dead because the love we have for one another in Christ brings deep sorrow when we are parted. Jesus wept at the grave of his friend, Lazarus. So, while we rejoice that the one we love has entered into the nearer presence of our Savior, our tears are shed in sympathy with those who mourn. Funerals provide opportunities to express the mixture of these feelings.

Funeral rites, in contrast to many other liturgical observances, often consist of a number of distinct liturgical events, and can be spread out over several days, weeks, or months. Prayers in the home, prayers in the presence of the body (whether in the home, in the church, in a funeral home, or elsewhere in cases of "lying in state"), "visitations" or "wakes," the reception of the body into the church, the public service (which may include the Eucharist), the committal of the body to the ground, the flames or the sea, the scattering or interring of ashes and/or the dedication of a marker at the place of burial, or prayers of remembrance at the anniversary of death, are all possible elements whereby the living mark the transition of one who has lived among us to the nearer presence of God.

From ancient times, the primary ministers of rites for the dead were family and loved ones of the deceased. Early in the history of the Church, Christians broadened this sense of family to include the congregation. Today, clergy and funeral directors serve and support the bereaved so that culturally appropriate pastoral rituals preceding public rites may be honored and protected.

Many cultures practice ancient customs like the visitation, or "wake," in which friends of the deceased call on those closest to her or him, praying in the presence of the body and offering con- solation or reminiscences of the deceased. This part of the ritual process may be an appropriate context for eulogies. In contrast, the burial liturgy rehearses Christ's saving work by which death was overcome for us. This Good News reminds us not only of the individual who has died but of the fact that all humanity must die. Through Christ's breaking the bonds of death we are confident that we will be raised in him. "Celebrations of a life" or personal anecdotes about the deceased, properly belong to the visitation or wake, or to a gathering after the burial. The sermon, in the burial liturgy, is a proclamation of the Gospel of the Resurrection.

Because of our Christian belief in Christ's incarnation and the bodily resurrection of the dead, it is it most appropriate that the body (or cremated remains) be present during all rites for the dead, except in cases where the corporal remains have been lost at sea or in similar accidents. In cases where the body (or cremated remains) cannot be present, prayers for the committal rite should be part of the burial liturgy. The proper locus for all public rites is the parish church except in unusual circumstances.

Through both the burial rite and the pastoral rituals surrounding death and burial, we acknowledge that the living are on this same journey toward the heart of the holy and undivided Trinity. As the ancient Eastern Orthodox memorial service proclaims, *Give rest, O Christ, to your servants with your saints, where sorrow and pain are no more, neither sighing, but life everlasting. All of us go down to the dust; yet even at the grave we make our song: Alleluia, alleluia, alleluia.*

Outline of the Rites

The resources included in this volume are intended to provide for a number of liturgical events marking the passage of an individual through death to life in the nearer presence of God. They supplement material in the 1979 Book of Common Prayer (pp. 462-466) and *Enriching our Worship 2* (pp. 96-116,131-146). Material from these sources may be used as needed to celebrate the life of the one who has died and to offer the bereaved consolation and hope of new life. **Note:** For ease of use and pastoral effectiveness, the material for the Burial of a Child from *Enriching Our Worship 2* has been included in this volume on pp. 39-56.

A. Preliminary Rites
In the days following a death, family members and others who knew the deceased, including members of the church, may gather at various times and places as the process of mourning begins. Several liturgical resources provide opportunity for prayer at some of these occasions:

◆ Prayers for a Vigil, pp. 13-17, may be used or adapted, along with material from Ministration at the Time of Death, BCP (pp. 462-66) and *Enriching Our Worship 2* (pp. 96-116), to gather family and friends in prayer. This may take place in a home, at a funeral home, at the church, or in any other suitable setting.

- A Vigil of the Resurrection, p. 15, may be used, or members of a congregation may keep watch with the body of the deceased if it is brought into the church some time before the burial liturgy.

- Reception of the Body, p. 21, is intended for use whenever the body is brought to the church. It may be used immediately prior to the public burial liturgy, or at an earlier time. Three alternatives are included in this volume, or the form from the BCP (pp. 466-467), may be used instead.

B. Order of Service for Burial

Ordinarily, a public liturgy for burial, with the body (or cremated remains) present, precedes the Committal. When pastorally desirable, however, the Committal may take place before the service in the church. The public liturgy follows the order of the Sunday Eucharist:

- *Gather in the Name of God.* Anthems are recited, drawing the congregation together as they remember God's love, mercy, and judgment, and the hope of resurrection with Christ. The gathering concludes with the collect of the day, joining the congregation in prayer for the one who has died and for those who mourn.

- *Proclaim and Respond to the Word.* One or more passages of scripture are read, including a reading from a Gospel if the Eucharist is to follow. The sermon proclaims the Gospel, bearing witness to the power of Christ's resurrection. After the sermon, the Apostles' Creed may be said, the baptismal proclamation of faith that unites the congregation with Christians of every time and place.

- *Pray for the World and the Church.* The Prayers of the People give thanks for the life of the one who has died, ask God's continuing mercy for the dead and the living, and

remember those who mourn. If desired, a Confession of Sin
and Absolution may follow the Prayers of the People.

◆ *Exchange of the Peace.* All present may greet one another
in the name of Christ.

◆ *Go forth in the name of Christ.* The congregation goes
forth in God's peace. This may take different forms,
depending on the circumstance.

◆ *Participate in the Sacrament of Christ's Body and Blood.*
The celebration of the Eucharist offers a foretaste of the
heavenly banquet as well as comfort and healing in the time
of mourning. All baptized persons present are invited to
receive the sacrament. A proper preface and postcommunion prayer emphasize hope and joy in Jesus Christ.

◆ *The Commendation* allows the congregation to entrust the
deceased into God's merciful care. This is suitable when the
body (or cremated remains) is present and the Committal
does not follow immediately in the church or churchyard.
The Commendation concludes with a blessing and dismissal, and the body is carried from the church as a hymn
or anthem is sung or recited.

◆ *The Committal* is appropriate when the body (or created
remains) is interred in the church building (i.e., a columbarium), churchyard, or cemetery. In this ritual, the congregation
commits the body to its resting place and to God's love. The
Committal concludes with a blessing and dismissal.

◆ A *Blessing* and *Dismissal* enable the congregation to depart
in peace, blessed by God, on those occasions where the
body (or cremated remains) is not present.

◆ A liturgy of burial of one who does not profess the Christian
faith may be used when the Church's usual burial rites do

not seem appropriate. The service follows the general outline above, omitting the celebration of the Eucharist: gathering, proclamation of the Word of God, prayer, and dismissal, including commendation.

C. The Committal

In the Committal rite, the congregation commits the body to its resting place and to God's love. Ordinarily, the body is lowered into the grave or placed in its final resting place before the rite begins. The materials in this volume may be adapted as needed for particular circumstances:

◆ One or more of the *Additional Prayers,* pp. 70-78, may be added before the blessing and dismissal.

◆ The *Committal under Special Circumstances,* p. 62, may be used for circumstances such as the transfer of a body from a funeral previously held elsewhere, or at a veterans' cemetery that does not permit graveside rites, or at a burial after temporary winter committal. This form includes options that permit a more substantial liturgy as well as prayers for special circumstances.

◆ *Prayers for the Committal of a Body at a Crematory,* pp. 84-86, are intended for use when loved ones gather at the time of cremation.

◆ Among the *Additional Prayers* is a prayer *"for temporary winter committal"* (p. 77), for use where frozen winter ground does not permit permanent interment at the time of the funeral.

◆ *The Consecration of a Grave* may be used before the service of Committal or at some other convenient time, if the grave is in a place not previously set apart for Christian burial.

D. After the Burial and Committal

The Church's pastoral care is important in the weeks and months following the death of a loved one. *A Service of Remembrance,* p. 87, may be used at the early anniversary of a death, and may also be used, as is customary in Eastern Orthodox traditions, on the fortieth day after the death. A family may pray this liturgy at home, or it may be used following a regular celebration of the Eucharist or Daily Office.

Concerning the Services

The death of a member of the Church should be reported as soon as possible to, and arrangements for the funeral should be made with, the member of the clergy or other person in charge of the congregation.

"Funeral rites, unlike most other liturgical observances, normally consist of a number of distinct liturgical events spread over a period of time, usually several days. They may include...prayers in the home, prayers in the presence of the body (whether in the home, or church or an undertaker's premises), the reception of the body at the church, a liturgy in an undertaker's chapel, a liturgy...in church, (and) the committal of the body..." (*Book of Alternative Services,* Anglican Church of Canada, p. 568).

Baptized Christians are properly buried from the church. The service should be held at a time when the congregation, *especially family and friends,* has an opportunity to be present.

The coffin is to be closed before the *main* burial service, regardless of location, and is to remain closed thereafter. It is expected that in the church the coffin will be covered with a pall, if available.

All or part of the Committal service may take place in the church. The Committal service may take place before the main service in the church, or prior to cremation.

A priest normally presides at the service. The Bishop, if present, presides at the Eucharist and leads the Commendation. In the absence of a priest, a deacon or lay reader may preside *at the Burial Office.*

When possible, the lessons from the Old Testament and the Epistles, *as well as the Prayers,* should be read by lay persons.

The presiding minister meets the body and goes before it into the church or toward the grave. When possible, a member of the congregation or other minister may lead the procession, carrying the paschal candle.

The anthems at the beginning of the service may be sung or said as the body is borne into the church, or during the entrance of the ministers, or by the presiding minister, standing in the accustomed place.

Vigils

Prayers for a Vigil in the Home or Elsewhere

Reception of the Body
The Prayer Book Liturgy, revised

It is appropriate that family and friends come together for prayer prior to the burial liturgy. Suitable Psalms, readings and prayers, such as those found in Enriching our Worship 2 *and the Lord's Prayer may be used. The Litany at the Time of Death (BCP, p. 462) may be used, or the following.*

Officiant

Jesus said: I am the resurrection and the life. Those who believe in me, even though they die, will live. *John 11:25*

Dear Friends in Christ:
Our Savior Jesus Christ said, "Come unto me, all you who labor and are burdened, and I will give you rest." Let us pray for *N.*, that *she* may rest from *her* labors, and enter into God's Sabbath rest. Loving God, receive *N.*, as *she* returns to you.
We commend our sister N.

Wash *her* in the living water of eternal life, and clothe *her* in *her* heavenly wedding garment.
We commend our sister N.

May *she* hear your words of invitation, "Come, you blessed of my Father."
We commend our sister N.

May *she* look upon you, face to face, and know the blessings of *her* eternal home.

We commend our sister N.

May angels surround *her* and saints welcome *her* in peace.
We commend our sister N.

The Officiant concludes

Gracious God, all who die in Christ live with you in eternity:
Receive N. into your heavenly dwelling. Let *her* heart and soul
now sing out to you, God of the living and the dead. This we ask
through Jesus Christ our redeemer, in the power of the Holy
Spirit. *Amen.*

*Here may be sung or said Nunc dimittis (BCP, p. 93) or some other appropriate
hymn, canticle, or song.*

Participants may be encouraged to share memories of the departed.

*The Officiant may continue with appropriate prayers from the section of
Additional Prayers (p. 70).*

Officiant

Let us pray.
God our Creator and Redeemer, in your power Christ conquered
death and entered into glory. Confident of that victory and claiming our Savior's promises, we entrust N. to your mercy in the
name of Jesus, who died and is alive, and reigns with you and the
Holy Spirit, now and for ever. *Amen.*

The Officiant then says

May God give you comfort and peace, light and joy, in this world
and the next; and the blessing of the eternal Trinity be with you
now, and always. *Amen.*

A Vigil of the Resurrection

If the body of a departed member is brought into the church the night before the funeral, it is desirable that members keep watch with the body. These prayers may be used, beginning with the closing of the coffin and recitation of Compline.

At each hour

Christ is risen from the dead, trampling down death, and giving life to those in the tomb.

Antiphon
Psalms – with antiphons as desired
Reading
The Lord's Prayer
Collect:
O God, who by the glorious resurrection of your Son Jesus Christ destroyed death and brought life and immortality to light: Grant that your servant N., being raised with him, may know the strength of his presence, and rejoice in his eternal glory; who with you and the Holy Spirit lives and reigns, one God, for ever and ever. *Amen.*

Other devotions and meditations may follow.

According to local custom, the body may be censed and/or sprinkled at the start of each hour.

Suggested hourly psalms and readings

Hour 1   *Antiphon*   Jesus came and stood among them and said, "Peace be with you." Alleluia.

           Psalms   1-18

           Reading   Isaiah 25:6-9

Hour 2   *Antiphon*   God led the people forth with gladness; God's chosen ones with shouts of joy. Alleluia.

           Psalms   19-32

           Reading   Isaiah 61:1-3

Hour 3   *Antiphon*   I know that my Redeemer lives, and shall stand at the last day upon the earth. Alleluia.

           Psalms   33-43

           Reading   Lamentations 3:22-26, 31-33

Hour 4   *Antiphon*   This Jesus, God raised up, and of that we are witnesses. Alleluia.

           Psalms   44-56

           Reading   Wisdom 3:1-5, 9

Hour 5   *Antiphon*   Thanks be to God, who gives us the victory through our Savior Jesus Christ. Alleluia.

           Psalms   57-70

           Reading   Job 19:21-27a

Hour 6   *Antiphon*   When Christ, who is our life appears, then you also will appear with him in glory. Alleluia.

           Psalms   71-80

           Reading   Romans 8:14-19, 34-35, 37-39

Hour 7	*Antiphon*	Fear not, I am the first and the last, and the living one; I died and behold, I am alive for evermore. Alleluia.
	Psalms	81-94
	Reading	1 Corinthians 15:20-26, 35-38, 42-44, 53-58

Hour 8	*Antiphon*	The Lamb in the midst of the throne will be their shepherd, and will guide them to springs of living water. Alleluia.
	Psalms	95-105
	Reading	2 Corinthians 4:16 – 5:9

Hour 9	*Antiphon*	My sheep hear my voice, and I give them eternal life. Alleluia.
	Psalms	106-118
	Reading	1 John 3:1-2

Hour 10	*Antiphon*	Blessed are those who are invited to the marriage supper of the Lamb. Alleluia.
	Psalm	119
	Reading	Revelation 7:9-17

Hour 11	*Antiphon*	Jesus said, if you loved me, you would have rejoiced, because I go to the Father. Alleluia.
	Psalms	120-139
	Reading	Revelation 21:2-7

Hour 12	*Antiphon*	The Spirit and the Bride say, "Come." Alleluia.
	Psalms	140-150
	Reading	John 6:37-40

Reception
of the Body

Reception of the Body

Reception of the Body
The Prayer Book Liturgy, revised

This rite may be used when the body is brought into the church. The Officiant meets the body saying

In the name of Jesus Christ, we receive the body of N. for burial. Let us pray with confidence to God, the giver of life, that N. will be raised to *her* place in the company of the saints.

Silence may be kept, after which the Officiant says

Deliver N., our Savior Jesus Christ, from all evil, and set *her* free from every bond, that *she* may feast with all your saints in light, where with the Father and the Holy Spirit, you live and reign, one God, for ever and ever. *Amen.*

Let us also pray for all who mourn, that they may cast all their care on our loving God, know the faithfulness of their Redeemer, and find solace in the divine compassion.

Silence may be kept, after which the Officiant says

Holy One, look with pity on the sorrows of your people for whom we pray. Remember them in mercy; comfort them with your loving kindness; lift up your countenance upon them, and give them your peace; through Jesus Christ our Savior. *Amen.*

Reception of the Body
from *Common Worship*

We receive the body of our *sister N.*, with confidence in God, the giver of life, who raised Jesus from the dead. Merciful God, may we who are baptized into the death of our Savior Jesus Christ be buried with him; that through the grave and gate of death we may pass to our joyful resurrection; through the One who died, was buried, and rose again for us, Jesus Christ our Redeemer. *Amen.*

As the coffin is covered with a pall, the Officiant may say

We are already God's children, but what we shall be has not yet been revealed. Yet we know that when Christ appears we shall be like him, for we shall see him as he is.   .

Reception of the Body
from *Renewing Worship*

The ministers meet the body at the entrance of the church. A pall may be placed on the coffin by family members, pall bearers, or other assisting ministers.

Officiant

Do you not know that all of us who have been baptized into Christ Jesus were baptized into his death? Therefore we have been buried with Jesus by baptism into death so that, just as Christ was raised from the dead by the glory of the Father, so we too might walk in newness of life. For if we have been united with Christ in a like death, we will certainly be united in a resurrection like his.

Water may be sprinkled on the coffin as a remembrance of Baptism.

Officiant

Eternal God, maker of heaven and earth,
who formed us from the dust of the earth,
who by your breath gave us life,
we glorify you.

Jesus Christ, the resurrection and the life,
who suffered death for all humanity,
who rose from the grave to open the way to eternal life,
we praise you.

Holy Spirit, author and giver of life,
the comforter of all who sorrow,
our sure confidence and everlasting hope,
we worship you.

To you, O Blessed Trinity, be glory and honor for ever and ever.
Amen.

The Burial
of the Dead

The Burial of the Dead

Those who are able shall stand while one or more of the following anthems are sung or said. A hymn, psalm, or other suitable anthem may be sung or said before or instead of the following

I am resurrection and I am life says the Lord. Those who believe in me, even though they die, will live, and everyone who lives and believes in me will never die.

For I know that my Redeemer lives, and at the last will stand upon the earth; and though worms destroy this body, yet in my flesh shall I see God, whom I shall see and my eyes behold, who is my friend and not a stranger. *Job 19:25-27*

We do not live to ourselves, and we do not die to ourselves. If we live, we live to the Lord, and if we die, we die to the Lord; so then, whether we live or die, we belong to the Lord. Happy from now on are those who die in the Lord! So it is, says the Spirit, for they rest from their labor.

or this

Blessed are those who mourn, for they will be comforted. This is indeed the will of my Father, that all who see the Son and believe in him may have eternal life; and I will raise them up on the last day. *Matthew 5:4, John 6:40*

God so loved the world that he gave his only Son, so that everyone who believes in him may not perish but may have eternal life. *John 3:16*

Since we believe that Jesus died and rose again, even so, through Jesus, God will bring with him those who have died. So we will be with the Lord for ever. Therefore encourage one another with these words. *1 Thessalonians 4:14,17b, 18 (Common Worship, pp. 275-293)*

or this

In the midst of life we are in death;
from whom can we seek help?
From you alone, O Lord,
who by our sins are justly angered.
Lord, you know the secrets of our hearts;
shut not your ears to our prayers,
but spare us, O Lord.
O worthy and eternal Judge,
do not let the pains of death
turn us away from you at our last hour.

Holy God,
Holy and Mighty,
Holy Immortal One,
have mercy upon us.

The Trisagion, above, may be repeated interspersed between verses. (Anthem, BCP, p. 492)

The Officiant may address the congregation, using these or other words, acknowledging the purpose of the gathering, and bidding their prayers for the deceased and the bereaved.

Officiant

We have come here today to remember before God our *sister N.*, to give thanks for *her* life; to commend *her* to God our merciful redeemer and judge; to commit *her* body to be *buried/cremated*, and to comfort one another in our grief.

Collects

Officiant

May God be with you.
And also with you.

Let us pray

A silence may be kept, followed by one of these collects

Eternal God, your mercy is without end, and your steadfast love
never ceases: Accept our prayers for N. and receive *her* into the
land of light and joy, into the company of your saints; for the
sake of Jesus Christ, our Redeemer, who lives and reigns with you
and the Holy Spirit, one God, now and for ever. *Amen.*

or this

God our Creator
your grace gives life to all;
receive N. into your keeping
and give *her* the new life
promised through Jesus Christ our Savior,
who once was dead and now lives
with you and the Holy Spirit,
for ever and ever. *Amen.*

or this

God the maker and Redeemer of all,
grant us with N. and all the faithful departed,
the sure benefits of Jesus' saving passion and glorious resurrection,
that in the last day, when you gather all into Christ,
we may enjoy the fullness of your promises;
through Jesus Christ, our Savior,
who lives and reigns with you in the unity of the Holy Spirit,
one God in glory everlasting. *Amen.*

or this

O God who brought us to birth,
and in whose arms we die,
comfort us in our grief and shock at the death of N.;
embrace us with your love,
give us hope in our confusion
and grace to let N. go into new life;
through Jesus Christ, our Savior. *Amen.*

or this

Hear us, Creator of all the living;
as N. is buried with Jesus the new Adam,
raise *her* from the dead in his resurrection
to dwell with you in eternity.
We grieve for N. with whom we shared our lives.
Reunite us with *her* on that day when we too shall pass
from death into the radiance of your eternal Easter,
and all stand rejoicing in your everlasting love. *Amen.*

or this

O God of grace and glory,
we remember N. before you
and thank you for giving *her* to us to know and to love
as a companion in our pilgrimage on earth.
In your compassion, console those who mourn.
Give us faith to see that death has been swallowed up
in the victory of Christ
so that we may live in confidence and hope
until, by your call, we are gathered
into the company of all your saints;
by the power of your Holy Spirit we pray. *Amen.*

The people sit.

The Liturgy of the Word

One or more of the Readings from the Book of Common Prayer (pp. 494-495), or from the following selections, may be used. If there is to be a Eucharist, a passage from the Gospel always concludes the Readings.

From the Old Testament

Isaiah 25:(6-7) 8-9 (The Lord will wipe away the tears)
Daniel 12:1-3 (Those who sleep in the dust shall awake)
Wisdom of Solomon 1:13-15 (God did not make death)
Job 14:7-9 (10-12) (Mortals die, and are laid low)

A suitable psalm, hymn, or canticle may follow. These psalms are appropriate.
42:1-7, 46, 90:1-12, 118:14-29, 121, 130, 139:1-11

Along with a psalm this antiphon may be used.
O deathless One: to those in darkness you appeared, raising
the fallen. O redeemer and our light: all glory be yours for ever.

From the New Testament

Romans 6:3-9 (10-11) (So we too might walk in newness of life)
Romans 8:14-19 (34-35, 37-39 (All who are led by the Spirit of
    God are children of God)
Romans 14:7-9 (And if we die, we die to the Lord)
1 Corinthians 15:20-26 (The last enemy...is death)
1 Corinthians 15:51-58 (Death has been swallowed up in victory)
2 Corinthians 5:1-9 (We walk by faith, not by sight)
1 Peter 1:3-9 (He has given us a new birth into a living hope)

A suitable psalm may follow.

The Gospel

Then, all standing, the Deacon or Minister appointed reads the Gospel, first saying

The Holy Gospel of our Savior Jesus Christ according to _____
Glory to you, Jesus Christ.

Matthew 11:25-30 (Come to me, all you that are weary)
Luke 24:13-16 (17-35) (The road to Emmaus)
John 20:11-18 (Mary encounters the risen Christ)

The Holy Gospel of our Redeemer.
Praise to you, Jesus Christ.

The Sermon

The Apostles' Creed may be said, all standing. The Officiant may introduce the Creed with these or similar words

In the assurance of eternal life given at Baptism, let us proclaim the faith and say

The Prayers

(For proposed forms see p. 79)

The service continues with the Prayers of the People. If the Eucharist is not celebrated, the Officiant concludes the Prayers by leading the Lord's Prayer. If the Committal follows immediately, the Lord's Prayer may be omitted here and included in the Committal.

When the Eucharist is not celebrated, the service continues with the Commendation or with the Committal.

In memorial services, with no remains present, the Officiant ends the service with selections from Additional Prayers (pp. 70-78) or other sources, and a final blessing.

At the Eucharist

The service continues with a Confession of Sin and Absolution, if desired, or the Peace and the Offertory. When the Eucharist is celebrated, all baptized persons present are welcome to receive Communion.

Preface of the Commemoration of the Dead, *BCP p. 382*

or one of these prefaces

Through Jesus Christ, our Savior, who has become for us the bridge and way into your perpetual life and light; and who is our hope, our strength, and our joy, even through the valley of the shadow of death, delivering us from fear and calling us to our eternal inheritance.

Through Jesus Christ, the pure brightness of the Everliving One, whose glory enfolds us in this world and the next, and who leads us into that place where every tear is wiped away, and we shall see you face to face.

In place of the usual postcommunion prayer, the following is said

Loving God,
we thank you that you have fed us
with the Body and Blood of our Savior Jesus Christ,
giving us a foretaste of your heavenly banquet.
We pray that this Sacrament
may be for us a comfort in affliction,
and a sign of our inheritance
in that place where there is no death,
neither sorrow nor crying,
but the joy of true homecoming,
through Jesus Christ our Redeemer. Amen.

If the body is not present, the service concludes with the (blessing and) dismissal. Unless the Committal follows immediately in the church, the following Commendation is used.

34

The Commendation

The Officiant and other ministers take their places at the body. Family members may join them.

This anthem or some other suitable anthem, or hymn, may be sung or said

Give rest, O Christ, to your servants with your saints,
where sorrow and pain are no more,
neither sighing, but life everlasting.

You only are immortal, the creator and maker of all; and we are
mortal, formed of the earth, and to earth shall we return. For so
you ordained when you created us, saying, "You are dust, and to
dust you shall return." All of us go down to the dust; yet even at
the grave we make our song: Alleluia, alleluia, alleluia.

Give rest, O Christ, to your servants with your saints,
where sorrow and pain are no more,
neither sighing, but life everlasting.

or this

Officiant

Let us commend N. to the mercy of God.

Silence may be kept.

God our Creator and Redeemer:
by your power Christ conquered death and entered into glory.
Confident of his victory and claiming his promises,
we entrust N. to your mercy

in the name of Jesus, who died and is alive
and reigns with you and the Holy Spirit,
now and for ever. Amen

Facing the body, the Officiant says

Merciful Savior, we commend N. to you. Receive *her* as a sheep
of your own fold, a lamb of your own flock, a sinner of your
own redeeming. Accept *her* into the arms of your mercy, into the
blessed rest of everlasting peace, and into the glorious company
of your saints. *Amen.*

If the Committal does not follow immediately, the following prayer is said

Blessed Jesus, Son of the Living God, we pray you to set your
passion, cross, and death between your judgment and our souls,
now and in the hour of our death. Give mercy and grace to the
living, pardon and peace to the dead; to your holy Church peace
and concord; and to us sinners everlasting life and glory; for with
the Father and the Holy Spirit you live and reign, one God, now
and for ever. *Amen.*

*The Officiant, or the Bishop, if present, may then bless the people, and a deacon
or other minister may dismiss them, saying*

Let us go forth in the name of Christ.
Thanks be to God.

*As the body is carried from the church, a hymn, or one or more of these
anthems may be said or sung.*

Christ is risen from the dead, trampling down death by death,
and giving life to those in the tomb.

The Sun of Righteousness is gloriously risen, giving light to those
who sat in darkness and in the shadow of death.

The Lord will guide our feet into the way of peace, having taken away the sin of the world. Christ will open the kingdom to all who believe in his Name, saying, Come, O blessed of my Father; inherit the kingdom prepared for you.

Into paradise may the angels lead you. At your coming may the martyrs receive you, and bring you into the holy city, Jerusalem.

or one of these canticles

The Song of Zechariah, *Benedictus*
The Song of Simeon, *Nunc Dimittis*
Christ our Passover, *Pascha nostrum*

Burial of a Child

Burial of a Child

Concerning the Service

The death of a member of the Church should be reported as soon as possible to, and arrangements for the funeral should be made in consultation with, the Minister of the Congregation.

Baptized Christians are properly buried from the church. The service should be held at a time when the congregation has opportunity to be present.

The coffin is to be closed before the service, and it remains closed thereafter. It is appropriate that it be covered with a pall or other suitable covering. If necessary, or if desired, all or part of the service of Committal may be said in the church. If preferred, the Committal service may take place before the service in the church. It may also be used prior to cremation.

A priest normally presides at the service. It is appropriate that the bishop, when present, preside at the Eucharist and pronounce the Commendation.

It is desirable that the Lesson from the Old Testament, and the Epistle, be read by lay persons.

When the services of a priest cannot be obtained, a deacon or lay reader may preside at the service.

It is customary that the celebrant meet the body and go before it into the church or towards the grave.

The anthems at the beginning of the service are sung or said as the body is borne into the church, or during the entrance of the ministers, or by the celebrant standing in the accustomed place.

When children die, it is usually long before their expected span of life. Often they die very suddenly and sometimes violently, whether as victims of abuse, gunfire, or drunken drivers, adding to the trauma of their survivors. The surprise and horror at the death of a child call for a liturgical framework that addresses these different expectations and circumstances.

Gather in the Name of God

All stand while one or more of the following is said or sung

He will feed his flock like a shepherd; he will gather the lambs in his arms, and carry them in his bosom. *Isaiah 40:11*

The eternal God is your refuge, and underneath are the everlasting arms. *Deuteronomy 33:27*

As a mother comforts her child, so I will comfort you. *Isaiah 66:13a*

When Israel was a child, I loved him.... it was I who taught Ephraim to walk, I took them up in my arms.... I led them with...bands of love. I was to them like those who lift infants to their cheeks. I bent down to them and fed them. *Hosea 11:1a, 3, 4*

For these things I weep; my eyes flow with tears.... But you, O Lord, reign for ever; your throne endures to all generations. *Lamentations 1:16a; 5:19*

Jesus said, Let the little children come to me, and do not stop them; for it is to such as these that the kingdom of heaven belongs. *Matthew 19:14*

For the Lamb at the center of the throne will be their shepherd, and he will guide them to springs of the water of life, and God will wipe away every tear from their eyes. *Revelation 7:17*

When all are in place, the Minister may address the congregation, acknowledging briefly the purpose of their gathering, and bidding their prayers for the deceased and the bereaved.

The Minister says one of the following Collects, first saying

	The Lord be with you.
People	And also with you.
Minister	Let us pray.

Silence

Holy God, your beloved Son took children into his arms and blessed them. Help us to entrust *N.* to your never failing loving-kindness. Comfort us as we bear the pain of *her/his* death, and reunite us in your good time in your Paradise; through Jesus Christ our Savior who lives and reigns with you and the Holy Spirit, one God, now and forever. *Amen.*

or this Collect for the family and all who grieve

Gracious God, we come before you this day in pain and sorrow. We grieve the loss of *N.*, a precious human life. Give your grace to those who grieve [especially *N.*], that they may find comfort in your presence and be strengthened by your Spirit. Be with this your family as they mourn, and draw them together in your healing love; in the name of the one who suffered, died, and rose for us, Jesus our Savior. *Amen.*

The Lessons

One or more of the following passages from Holy Scripture is read. If the Eucharist is celebrated, a passage from the Gospel always concludes the Readings.

From the Old Testament

2 Samuel 12:16-23 (the death of David's child)
Isaiah 65:17-20, 23-25 (I am about to create new heavens and
    a new earth)
Isaiah 66:7-14 (As a mother comforts her child, so will I comfort you)
Jeremiah 31:15-17 (Rachel weeping for her children)

Psalms 23; 42:1-7

From the New Testament

Romans 8:31-39 (Who will separate us from the love of Christ?)
1 Thessalonians 4:13-14,18 (We do not want you to be
    uninformed about those who have died)
1 John 3:1-2 (See what love the Father has given us)

Psalms 121; 139:7-12; 142:1-6

The Gospel

Matthew 5:1-10 (Blessed are those who mourn)
Matthew 18:1-5, 10-14 (this child is the greatest in the kingdom)
Mark 10:13-16 (Let the little children come to me); see also
Matthew 19:13-15; Luke 18:15-17
John 10:11-16 (I am the good shepherd)

The Sermon

The Apostles' Creed may then be said, all standing. The Celebrant may introduce the Creed with these or similar words

In the assurance of eternal life given at Baptism, let us proclaim our faith and say,

Celebrant and People

I believe in God, the Father almighty,
>   creator of heaven and earth.
I believe in Jesus Christ, his only Son, our Lord.
>   He was conceived by the power of the Holy Spirit
>   and born of the Virgin Mary.
>   He suffered under Pontius Pilate,
>   was crucified, died, and was buried.
>   He descended to the dead.
>   On the third day he rose again.
>   He ascended into heaven,
>   and is seated at the right hand of the Father.
>   He will come again to judge the living and the dead.

I believe in the Holy Spirit,
>   the holy catholic Church,
>   the communion of saints,
>   the forgiveness of sins,
>   the resurrection of the body,
>   and the life everlasting. Amen.

The service continues with the Prayers. If the Eucharist is not celebrated, the Lord's Prayer concludes the intercessions.

The Prayers of the People

The Deacon or other person appointed says

In the peace of God, let us pray, responding "O God, have mercy."

In the assurance of your mercy, in thanksgiving for the life of your child N., and in confident expectation of the resurrection to eternal life, we pray

Here and after every petition, the people respond

O God, have mercy.
Remember N.'s parents, N. N. Help them to hold each other in their hearts, that this sorrow may draw them together and not tear them apart, we pray

Remember N.'s brother(s) N., N. and sister(s) N., N., that *they/he/she* may be enfolded in love, comforted in fear, honored in *their/his/her* grief, and kept safe, we pray

Remember all the family and friends of N., that they may know the consolation of your love, and may hold N. in their love all the days of their lives, we pray

Support them in their grief, and be present to all who mourn, we pray

Teach us to be patient and gentle with ourselves and each other as we grieve, we pray

Help us to know and accept that we will be reunited at your heavenly banquet, we pray

Finally, our God, help us become co-creators of a world in which children are happy, healthy, loved and do not know want or hunger, we pray

The Minister concludes the prayers with this Collect

Compassionate God, your ways are beyond our understanding, and your love for those whom you create is greater by far than ours; comfort all who grieve for this child N. Give them the faith to endure the wilderness of bereavement and bring them in the fullness of time to share with N. the light and joy of your eternal presence; through Jesus Christ our Lord. *Amen.*

When the Eucharist is not to be celebrated, the service continues with the Commendation or with the Committal.

At the Eucharist

In place of the usual postcommunion prayer, the following is said

Almighty God, we thank you that in you great love you have fed us with the spiritual food and drink of the Body and Blood of your Son Jesus Christ, and have given us a foretaste of your heavenly banquet. Grant that this Sacrament may be to us a comfort in affliction, and a pledge of our inheritance in that kingdom where there is no death, neither sorrow nor crying, but the fullness of joy with all your saints; through Jesus Christ our Savior. Amen.

The Commendation

The Celebrant and other ministers take their places at the body.

This anthem, or some other suitable anthem, or a hymn, may be sung or said.

Give rest, O Christ, to your servant(s) with your saints,
where sorrow and pain are no more,
neither sighing, but life everlasting.

You only are immortal, the creator and maker of mankind; and we are mortal, formed of the earth, and to earth shall we return. For so did you ordain when you created me, saying, "You are dust, and to dust your shall return." All of us go down to the dust, yet even at the grave we make our song: Alleluia, alleluia, alleluia.

Give rest, O Christ, to your servant(s) with your saints,
where sorrow and pain are no more,
neither sighing, but life everlasting.

The minister, facing the body, says

We commend N. to the mercy of God, our maker, redeemer, and comforter.

N., our companion in faith and fellow child of Christ, we entrust you to God. Go forth from this world in the love of God who created you, in the mercy of Jesus who died for you, in the power of the Holy Spirit who receives and protects you. May you rest in peace and rise in glory, where pain and grief are banished, and life and joy are yours for ever. *Amen.*

or this

Into your hands, O merciful Savior, we commend your servant N. Acknowledge, we humbly beseech you, a sheep of your own fold, a lamb of your own flock, a sinner of your own redeeming. Receive *him* into the arms of your mercy, into the blessed rest of everlasting peace, and into the glorious company of the saints in light. *Amen.*

The Blessing and Dismissal follow.

The Committal

One or more of the following anthems is sung or said

They are before the throne of God,
and worship him day and night within his temple,
and the one who is seated on his throne will shelter them.
They will hunger no more and thirst no more;
the sun will not strike them, nor any scorching heat;
for the Lamb at the center of the throne will be their shepherd,
and he will guide them to springs of the water of life,
and God will wipe away every tear from their eyes.
Revelation 7:15-17

or this

See, the home of God is among mortals. He will dwell with them
    as their God;
they will be his peoples, and God himself will be with them;
he will wipe away every tear from their eyes. Death will be no more;
mourning and crying and pain will be no more, for the first
    things have passed away.
Those who conquer will inherit these things, and I will be their
    God, and they will be my children.
Revelation 21:3b-4, 7

Before the following prayer, the coffin may be lowered into the grave.
Then, while earth is cast upon the coffin, the minister says these words

In sure and certain hope of the resurrection to eternal life through
our Lord Jesus Christ, we commend to Almighty God our *brother*
N., and we commit *his* body to the ground;* earth to earth, ashes
to ashes, dust to dust. The Lord bless *him* and keep *him*, the Lord
make his face to shine upon *him* and be gracious to *him*, the Lord
lift up his countenance upon *him* and give *him* peace. *Amen.*

* *Or* the deep, *or* the elements, *or* its resting place.

Then shall be sung or said

Jesus said to his friends, "You have pain now; but I will see you again, and your hearts will rejoice, and no one will take your joy from you." *John 16:22*

Then the minister says

The Lord be with you.

People   And also with you.

Minister   Let us pray.

Loving God, we stand before you in pain and sadness. You gave the gift of new life, and now it has been taken from us. Hear the cry of our hearts for the pain of our loss. Be with us as we struggle to understand the mystery of life and death. Receive *N.* in the arms of your mercy, to live in your gracious and eternal love, and help us to commit ourselves to your tender care. In Jesus' name we pray. *Amen.*

or this

God, you have loved us into being. Hear our cries at our loss of *N.* Move us from the shadow of death into the light of your love and peace in the name of Mary's child, Jesus the risen one. *Amen.*

Here one or more of the additional prayers may be said. Then the Lord's Prayer may be said.

As our Savior Christ has taught us, we now pray,

And now, as our Savior Christ has taught us, we are bold to say,

Officiant and People

Officiant and People

Our Father in heaven,	Our Father, who art in heaven,
hallowed be your Name,	hallowed be thy Name,
your kingdom come,	thy kingdom come,
your will be done,	thy will be done,
on earth as in heaven.	on earth as it is in heaven.
Give us today our daily bread.	Give us this day our daily bread.
Forgive us our sins	And forgive us our trespasses,
as we forgive those	as we forgive those
who sin against us.	who trespass against us.
Save us from the time of trial,	And lead us not into temptation,
and deliver us from evil.	but deliver us from evil.
For the kingdom, the power,	For thine is the kingdom,
and the glory are yours,	and the power, and the glory
now and for ever. Amen.	for ever and ever. Amen.

The Blessing follows.

The God of peace, who brought again from the dead our Lord Jesus Christ, the great Shepherd of the sheep, through the blood of the everlasting covenant: Make you perfect in every good work to do his will, working in you that which is well-pleasing in his sight; through Jesus Christ, to whom be glory for ever and ever. *Amen.*

The service concludes with this Dismissal

Since we believe that Jesus died and rose again, so will it be for those who have died: God will bring them to life with Jesus. Alleluia.

Go in peace in the name of Christ.

Additional Prayers

The Death of an Infant

God our Creator, you called into being this fragile life, which had seemed to us so full of promise: give to N., whom we commit to your care, abundant life in your presence, and to us, who grieve for hopes destroyed, courage to bear our loss; through Jesus Christ our Savior. *Amen.*

For a Miscarriage

O God, who gathered Rachel's tears over her lost children, hear now the sorrow and distress of N. [and N.] for the death of *their/her/his* expected child; in the darkness of loss, stretch out to *them/her/him* the strength of your arm and renewed assurance of your love; through your own suffering and risen Child Jesus. *Amen.*

For a Stillbirth or Child Who Dies Soon after Birth

Heavenly Father, your love for all children is strong and enduring. We were not able to know N. as we hoped. Yet you knew *her/him* growing in *her/his* mother's womb, and *she/he* is not lost to you. In the midst of our sadness, we thank you that N. is with you now. *Amen.*

For a Mother Whose Child has Died Near Birth

Loving God, we thank you that in your mercy you brought your daughter N. through childbirth in safety. We pray that N. [and N.] will know your support in this time of trouble and enjoy your protection always; through Jesus Christ our Savior. *Amen.*

For a Child Who Dies by Violence

Loving God, Jesus gathered your little ones in his arms and blessed them. Have pity on those who mourn for N., an innocent slaughtered by the violence of our fallen world. Be with us as we struggle with the mysteries of life and death; in our pain, bring your comfort, and in our sorrow, bring your hope and your promise of new life, in the name of Jesus our Savior. *Amen.*

or this

God our deliverer, gather our horror and pity for the death of your child N. into the compass of your wisdom and strength, that through the night we may seek and do what is right, and when morning comes trust ourselves to your cleansing justice and new life; through Christ our Savior. *Amen.*

or this

God, do not hide your face from us in our anger and grief for the death of N. Renew us in hope that your justice will roll down like mighty waters and joy spring up from the broken ground in a living stream; through Jesus our Savior. *Amen.*

For One Who Has Killed

Holy God, we lift into the light of your justice N. [the one] who has taken the life of your child N. Where our hearts are stone return to us hearts of flesh; that grief may not swallow us up, but new life find us through Jesus the crucified, with whom we are raised by your power. *Amen.*

For Those Who Mourn

God of compassion and strength: keep safe the soul of your child N., whose moment of pain and fear is past. Send your healing to N. [and N.] and all who mourn, that their suffering may find peace and resolution within your love, whose Spirit gives life in Christ our Savior. *Amen.*

or this

Most loving God: the death of your Son has opened to us a new and living way. Give us hope to overcome our despair; help us to surrender N. to your keeping, and let our sorrow find comfort in your care; through the name and presence of Jesus our Savior. *Amen.*

or this

God, as Mary stood at the foot of the cross, we stand before you with broken hearts and tearful eyes. Keep us mindful that you know our pain, and free us to see your resurrection power already at work in N.'s life. In your time, raise us from our grief as you have raised N. to eternal life; through Jesus Christ our Savior. *Amen.*

or this

Merciful God, you grant to children an abundant entrance into your kingdom. In your compassion, comfort those who mourn for N., and grant us grace to conform our lives to *her/his* innocence and faith, that at length, united with *her/him*, we may stand in your presence in the fullness of joy; for the sake of Jesus Christ. *Amen.*

For a Child Dead by Suicide

Out of the depths we cry to you, merciful God, for your child N.,
dead by *her/his* own hand. Meet our confusion with your peace,
our anger with forgiveness, our guilt with mercy, and our sorrow
with consolation. Help us acknowledge the mystery that our lives
are hid with Christ in you, whose compassion is over all whom
you have made. *Amen.*

or this

All-knowing and eternal God, come to our help as we mourn for
N., dead by *her/his* own hand. We know only in part, we love
imperfectly, and we fail to ease one another's pain as you intend.
But you are the God whose property is always to have mercy, and
so we put our trust in you and ask the courage to go on; through
our Savior Christ, who suffered for us, and whom you raised to
new life. *Amen.*

Hymns Appropriate for the Burial of a Child

The Hymnal 1982

482	Lord of all hopefulness, Lord of all joy
490	I want to walk as a child of the light
620	Jerusalem, my happy home
645, 646	The King of love my shepherd is
676	There is a balm in Gilead
712	Dona nobis pacem

Wonder, Love, and Praise

787	We are marching in the light of God
800	Precious Lord, take my hand
810	You who dwell in the shelter of the Lord (Eagle's wings)
813	Way, way, way

Lift Every Voice and Sing II

8	Deep river
72	Just a closer walk with thee
91	Give me Jesus
103	Steal away
106	Take my hand
141	Shall we gather at the river
207	We'll understand it better by and by
213	Children of the heavenly Father
218	Jesus loves me, this I know
279	The Lord is my shepherd (Psalm 23)

Lutheran Book of Worship

474	Children of the heav'nly Father

The Committal

The Committal

It is customary that the coffin is lowered into the grave, or placed in its resting place. The following anthem, or one of those on p. 49, is said or sung.

Everyone the Father gives to me will come to me;
I will never turn away anyone who believes in me.
The One who raised Jesus Christ from the dead
will also give life to our mortal bodies
through the indwelling Spirit.
My heart therefore, is glad, and my spirit rejoices;
my body also shall rest in hope.
You will show me the path of life;
in your presence there is fullness of joy,
and in your right hand are the pleasures for evermore.

Then, while earth is cast upon the coffin, the Officiant says these words

In sure and certain hope of the resurrection to eternal life through Jesus Christ our Savior, we commend N. to *her* loving God, and we commit *her* body/remains to the [ground, the deep, the elements, its resting place] earth to earth, ashes to ashes, dust to dust. The Lord bless *her* and keep *her*, the Lord make his face to shine upon *her* and be gracious to *her*, the Lord lift up his countenance upon *her* and give *her* peace. *Amen.*

or this

We have entrusted N. to God's mercy, and we commit *her* body to the ground [or to be cremated], earth to earth, ashes to ashes, dust to dust; in sure and certain hope of the resurrection to eternal life through our Savior Jesus Christ, who will transform our bodies so that they may be conformed to his glorious body. To Christ be glory for ever and ever. *Amen.*

or this

Holy God, Holy and Powerful, Holy Immortal One,
by the death and burial of Jesus your anointed
you have destroyed the power of death
and awakened the dead into your true and eternal life.
Keep N. whose *body* we now lay to rest in the company
    of your saints.
And at the last raise *her* up to share with all the faithful
the endless joy and peace won through the victory of Christ
    our Savior,
who lives and reigns with you and the Holy Spirit,
    to the ages of ages. *Amen.*

When the Committal immediately follows the Eucharist, the Lord's Prayer may be omitted here.

May God be with you.
And also with you.

Let us pray.

The Lord's Prayer

Other prayers may be added.

Then may be said

Rest eternal grant to *her*, O God;
And let light perpetual shine upon her.
May *her* soul, and the souls of all the departed,
through the mercy of God, rest in peace. *Amen.*

Jesus, Savior of the world,
be gracious to us.
By your incarnation and nativity,
be gracious to us.
By your prayers and tears,
be gracious to us.
By your grief and anguish,
be gracious to us.
By your cross and suffering,
be gracious to us.
By your atoning death,
be gracious to us.
By your rest in the grave,
be gracious to us.
By your triumphant resurrection,
be gracious to us.
By your presence with your people,
be gracious to us.
By your promise of your coming at the end of the ages,
be gracious to us.

The God of peace, who brought again from the dead our Lord
Jesus Christ, the great Shepherd of the sheep, through the blood of
the everlasting covenant: Make you perfect in every good work to
do his will, working in you that which is well-pleasing in his sight;
through Jesus Christ, to whom be glory for ever and ever. *Amen.*

Go in peace. The souls of all the faithful departed are in the
hands of God. Alleluia.

Thanks be to God. Alleluia.

or this

Alleluia, Christ is risen.
The Lord is risen indeed. Alleluia.

Committal under Special Circumstances

On some occasions, a Committal rite needs to be more substantial, or to allow for particular circumstances such as the transfer of a body from a burial liturgy previously held elsewhere, or at one of the many veterans' cemeteries that do not permit graveside rites.

The Officiant may begin with this or other suitable anthems.

God so loved the world that he gave his only Son, so that everyone who believes in him may not perish but may have everlasting life.

or this

Grace and peace to you from our Savior Jesus Christ.

Let us pray.

Gracious God, you alone are the source of all life,
may your life-giving Spirit flow through us,
so that we may be ministers of your compassion to one another;
in our sorrow give us the calm of your peace,
kindle our hope,
and in your good time,
let our grief give way to joy,
through Jesus Christ our Deliverer. *Amen.*

A portion of scripture from the burial rite may be read.

A homily or hymn may follow.

When the burial liturgy has taken place elsewhere, the Officiant may say these or similar words

From the hands and prayers of our sisters and brothers in Christ in _____, we receive the body/remains of N. for burial. May God comfort all who mourn and strengthen our bonds of love in the body of Christ.

At locations where graveside services are prohibited, the following may be said

In sure and certain hope of the resurrection to eternal life through our Savior Jesus Christ, we commend N. to *her* merciful God. Grant that *her* body/remains may rest in peace, awaiting *her* last call to service; and that we and all who worship here may offer our humble thanks for those who have fought the good fight [and faithfully lived in service of their country], and who now wear the crown given us by the Victor over death, Jesus our Redeemer. *Amen.*

If the body is being committed to the earth immediately, standing before the grave, columbarium, or crematory door, the Officiant says

In sure and certain hope of the resurrection to eternal life through Jesus Christ our Savior, we commend N. to *her* loving God, and we commit *her* body/remains to the [ground, the deep, the elements, its resting place] earth to earth, ashes to ashes, dust to dust. The Lord bless *her* and keep *her*, the Lord make his face to shine upon *her* and be gracious to *her*, the Lord life up his countenance upon *her* and give *her* peace. *Amen.*

or this

We have entrusted N. to God's mercy, and we commit *her* body to the ground [or to be cremated], earth to earth, ashes to ashes, dust to dust; in sure and certain hope of the resurrection to eternal life through our Savior Jesus Christ, who will transform our bodies so that they may be conformed to his glorious body, who died, was buried, and rose again for us. To Christ be glory for ever and ever. *Amen.*

or this

Holy God, Holy and Mighty, Holy Immortal One,
by the death and burial of Jesus your anointed,
you have destroyed the power of death
and awakened the dead into your true and eternal life.
Keep N. whose body we now lay to rest in the company
    of your saints.
And at the last raise *her* up to share with all the faithful
the endless joy and peace won through the victory of Christ
    our Savior;
who lives and reigns with you and the Holy Spirit, one God,
unto ages of ages. Amen.

The Committal continues with the Salutation and Lord's Prayer, p. 60.

The Consecration of a Grave

If the grave is in a place not previously set apart for Christian burial, the priest may use the following prayer, either before the service of Committal, or at some other convenient time.

God of time and eternity,
whose hands have shaped the universe in love
and who makes all ground holy:
Bless this *ground* to be for us a place of sacred memory
where the bodies of those we love are laid
in hope of your resurrecting call
and in confidence of your unfailing love and mercy
shown to us in Jesus Christ the risen Savior. *Amen.*

or this

God of the living and the dead, the body of Jesus was laid in a
tomb in a garden: Bless this grave, and grant that N., whose
body/remains is [to be] buried here, may be with Christ in paradise,
in whose Name we pray. *Amen.*

or this

Bless this grave
as the place where the body of N. may rest in peace,
through Christ, who is the resurrection and the life,
who died and is alive,
and reigns with you and the Holy Spirit
now and for ever. *Amen.*

Burial of One Who Does Not Profess the Christian Faith

When, for pastoral consideration, none of the Church's usual burial rites is appropriate, the following may be used.

The service begins with one or more of the following anthems

Blessed are they who mourn; for they shall be comforted.

God is our refuge and strength, a very present help in trouble.

The eternal God is your refuge and underneath are the
    everlasting arms.

Peace I leave with you, my peace I give to you;
    not as the world gives, give I to you.

Let not your hearts be troubled, neither let them be afraid.

Officiant

May God be with you.
And also with you.
Let us pray.

Merciful God, our only help in time of need,
be with your people in their trouble.
Give them hope,
and nourish them with your loving-kindness;
receive N. in *her* death
and take *her* into your holy keeping,
for your mercy's sake. *Amen.*

Liturgy of the Word

From the Old Testament
Ecclesiastes 3:1-8
   (For everything there is a season)
Lamentations 3:22-26 (31-33)
   (The Lord is good to those who wait for him)
Wisdom of Solomon 3:1-5
   (The souls of the righteous are in the hand of God)

One or more of the following psalms may be sung or said
   39
   91:1-12
   103
   116

From the New Testament
2 Corinthians 5:1-9
   (We have a building from God)
Revelation 21:2-7
   (Behold, I make all things new)

One or more of the following psalms may be sung or said
   23
   27
   106
   130
   139

From the Gospels
Matthew 5:1-10 (The Beatitudes)
John 14:1-4 (In my Father's house are many rooms)
John 14:25-29 (Peace I leave with you)

A homily follows.

A hymn or anthem may be sung.

One of the forms of the Prayers of the People, pp. 79-83, may follow, concluding with a suitable prayer such as this

Gracious God,
to whom no prayer is offered without hope of mercy:
give us your consolation
as we come to you under the shadow of our affliction.
Strengthen our faith
in your unfailing compassion;
deliver us from bitterness and despair,
and help us to know your peace,
which passes all understanding. *Amen.*

Other prayers may be offered.

Commendation

Into your hands, Immortal One, we commend N.
Of your infinite goodness, wisdom, and power,
work in *her* the wonderful purpose of your perfect will,
for your mercies' sake. *Amen.*

The Officiant may conclude the service with this or another blessing

Now unto the One who is able to keep you from falling,
and to present you faultless before the Divine Presence,
to the only wise God, our refuge and our rock,
be glory, dominion, and power,
now and for ever. *Amen.*

Committal

At the grave, or place of final prayers, the service may begin with the following

In the midst of life we are in death; to whom may we turn for
help but to you, most merciful God.

Then may follow this, or some other committal prayer.

You only are immortal, the creator and maker of all,
and we are mortal, formed of the earth, and to earth shall we return.
For so you ordained when you created me, saying,
"You are dust and to dust you shall return."
All of us go down to the dust,
yet even at the grave we make our song: Alleluia, alleluia, alleluia.

Additional Prayers

Eternal God, redeemer of those who have died in Christ and with whom the souls of the faithful are in joy and felicity: We give you thanks for the good examples of all who have gone before us, who, having finished their course in faith, now find rest and refreshment. May we, with all who have died in the faith of your holy Name, find fulfillment and bliss in your eternal and everlasting glory; through Jesus Christ, who has won the victory. *Amen.*

Eternal God, whose days are without end, and whose mercies cannot be numbered: Help us to be conscious of the brevity and uncertainty of all human life. May your Holy Spirit lead us all our days, so that when we shall have served you in our time, we may be gathered to our ancestors, having a good conscience, in the communion of the Catholic Church, in the confidence of a sure faith, in the comfort of a holy hope, in favor with you, our God, and at peace with the world. This we ask in the name of Jesus Christ our Savior. *Amen.*

God of the saints, we bless your holy name for all who have finished their course in faith: for the Blessed Virgin Mary, for _____, matriarchs, patriarchs, prophets and martyrs; and for all your people, known and unknown; and we pray that, encouraged by their example, upheld by their prayers, and strengthened by their companionship on the way, we may also share in the inheritance of your saints, through Jesus Christ our Redeemer. *Amen.*

Jesus our Savior, by your death you took away the sting of death: Grant that we may follow in faith where you have led the way, so that we may fall asleep peacefully in you and awake in your likeness, for your tender mercies' sake. *Amen.*

Creator of all, we pray for those we love, but see no longer: Grant them your peace; let light perpetual shine upon them; and, in your loving wisdom and gracious power, work in them the divine purpose of your perfect will; through Jesus Christ, who rose from the dead that we might share your life. *Amen.*

Merciful God, Father of our Savior Jesus Christ who is the Resurrection and the Life: Raise us from the death of sin to the life of righteousness, that when we die we may rest in our Redeemer, and at the Last Day may receive the blessing that your well-beloved shall then proclaim: "Come, you blessed of my Father, receive the kingdom prepared for you from the beginning of the world." Grant this for the sake of Jesus Christ, our Mediator and Advocate. *Amen.*

Gracious God, grant to all who are bereaved the spirit of faith and courage, that they may have strength to face the future with assurance and patience, not as those who are without hope, but in thankful remembrance of your loving-kindness, and in the joyful expectation of eternal life in your presence, with those they love. This we ask in the name of Jesus Christ, risen in glory. *Amen.*

Eternal God, fountain of mercies and giver of comfort: Deal graciously with all who mourn, that casting their care on you, they may know the power of your love; through Jesus Christ, our Hope and our Peace. *Amen.*

Remember N., Holy God, with the favor you have shown to your people in ages past, that *she* may increase in the knowledge and love of you and go from strength to strength in a new life of perfect service in your eternal reign; through Jesus Christ, the Servant and Savior of all. *Amen.*

Additional Prayers from other sources

For the deceased

Gracious God,
nothing in death or life,
in the world as it is or the world as it shall be,
nothing in all creation can separate us from your love.
We commend N. into your loving care.
Enfold *her* in the arms of your mercy.
Bless *her* in *her* dying and in *her* rising again in you.
Bless those whose hearts are filled with sadness,
that they too may know the hope of resurrection;
for the sake of our Savior Jesus Christ. *Amen.*

Most loving God,
the death and resurrection of Jesus
have opened for us a new and living way.
Give us hope to overcome our fear;
help us to surrender N. to your keeping
and let our sorrow find comfort in your care,
through Jesus Christ, our Redeemer. *Amen.*

Gentle God,
N. has come by a hard and painful road
to the valley of death.
Lead *her* now to the place where there is no pain.
For the sake of Jesus, who suffered for us. *Amen.*

N. may Christ give you rest in the land of the living
and open the gates of Paradise for you;
may God receive you as a citizen of the Kingdom,
and grant you forgiveness of your sins:
for you were Christ's friend. *Amen.*

For those who mourn

Gracious God, you alone are the source of all life.
May your life-giving Spirit flow through us,
so that we may be ministers of your compassion to one another;
in our sorrow give us the calm of your peace,
and kindle our hope,
and in your good time,
let our grief give way to joy,
through Jesus Christ our Deliverer. *Amen.*

A commendation

Merciful God,
into whose hands Jesus committed his Spirit
at the last hour,
into your hands we now commend N.,
that death may be for *her* the gate
to life and peace with you;
through Jesus Christ, our Savior. *Amen.*

God of all consolation,
in your unending love and mercy
you turn the darkness of death
into the dawn of new life.
Jesus, by dying for us, conquered death
and by rising again, restored us to eternal life:
let us go forward to meet our Redeemer
so that after our life on earth,
we may be united with N., and all our brothers and sisters,
where every tear is wiped away and all things are made new;
through Jesus Christ our Savior. *Amen.*

For all present

God's eternal Word, the Father's only-begotten,
for love of us was born from Mary's womb.
A child of flesh and blood, he grew with us,
labored beside us, feeling our joy and pain,
and preached the kingdom of God come near.
All living things must return to earth, so Jesus died.
The Holy One of God gave himself up to death.
Yet the grave could not hold him.
Christ broke death's bonds and rose on the third day:
"Why do you look for the living among the dead?
Christ is not in the tomb. Christ is risen as he told us."
So we shall be raised in Christ, incorruptible.
Do not look for the risen among graves.
Their stones are a reminder
that those who followed Christ on earth now worship God for ever.
Others will learn the same of us
when we who stand here now will join with those
who entered glory before us, and sing
praise to the holy Trinity, one God,
alive through all the ages. *Amen.*

For one who has died in Military or Public Safety service

Holy God, in your creating power
you renew the whole face of the earth
and call those who sleep in death to awake
to new life with you.
Wake this sleeper, N.
who has died [in time of conflict]
after giving *her* dedicated service
for us, and [*her* country, state, city].
Keep *her* in that place of light and safety
where fear and dread are banished
and where your beloved children enjoy your full Presence

74

until that time when they are united again
with all those whom they love.
We ask this in your holy and life-giving Name. *Amen.*

God the King of Glory, in whose hands are the living and the
dead: We give you thanks for [N. and] all those who have laid
down their lives in the service of our country. Grant them your
mercy and the light of your presence; and give us a sense of your
will and purpose, that we may understand that the work you
have begun in them will be perfected through Jesus Christ, the
Prince of Peace, in whom all strife is resolved. *Amen.*

*At the reception of a body of one who has died in Military or
Public Safety service*

Have mercy, Lord, have mercy,
on our honored dead whom we receive in your name.
We praise you for *his* life,
for the gift of *his* courage and service,
for *his* companionship in the company of
　　[soldiers, fellow officers, etc.]
and for *his* unique presence in the world.
We mourn *his* passing.
We salute *his* sacrifice.
We pray for those who will grieve for *him.*
Strong Savior, raise *him* up in strength,
in wholeness and beauty,
to share with you the eternal life that you have promised
to all who put their trust in you.
In your holy Name we pray. *Amen.*

For one of another or unknown faith

God of power and mercy, you hold the universe in your hands
and all that breathes has life from you.

We commend to you this person
whose faith is known to you
and whose heart's prayers you have heard in life.
We give honor to *his* body
which was marvelously made,
to all the relationships that held *him,*
and to those who will mourn *him.*
We trust that all those whom you have created
will never be lost to you.
God whose names are many,
whose mystery is vast,
and whose love endures for ever. *Amen.*

For the burial of an unbeliever

Merciful God, you draw us to yourself
and we are never distant from your love.
You alone know us through and through,
judge our sin, and take the measure of our faith;
only you know the goodness that is in us,
our doubt, our hope.
We commend to you our companion N.,
whom you love,
whom you made to explore your mystery
and to come home to you,
where *she* may rejoice to see you face to face
and know as *she* is known. *Amen.*

Merciful God,
whose hand holds us fast in the uttermost parts of the sea
and in the highest corners of heaven:
Hear our prayers for N.,
whose life was a gift and a treasure to those who love him;
we entrust *him* to your untiring care –
you who read the hidden depths of our hearts –
knowing your power to do better things for all of us

than we can hope or imagine,
through Jesus Christ,
who descended to the dead to raise to new life those who
    had been lost,
and whose love for us is unceasing. *Amen.*

For temporary winter committal

Eternal God, our time is in your hands.
We commend the body of N. to you
to rest until Spring and the greening of the earth allows burial.
Through the Winter frost,
help us to cherish our memories of N.,
remembering that all of us await with hope
our resurrection life,
in Jesus Christ our Redeemer. *Amen.*

For the funeral of a member of an inter-faith family

Welcoming God:
You call your Church to love and serve all people
and to honor the image of you, our Creator, in them:
In our several faiths,
we gather to give thanks for the life of [your child] N.,
whose departure we grieve,
whose good works and heritage we celebrate,
whose memories are woven into our hearts.
Holding the future in hope,
and the past in compassion and gratitude,
we join our various prayers
with those of God's people of every time and every place,
through Jesus Christ and your Holy Spirit. *Amen.*

A prayer of St. Anselm

Jesus, sweet Lord,
are you not also a mother?
Truly, you are a mother,
the mother of all mothers,
who tasted death
in your longing to give life to your children. *Amen.*

Ancient Mozarabic prayer

Hear us, O never-failing Light,
Lord our God, our only Light, the Fountain of Light,
the Light of your angels, thrones, dominions,
principalities, powers, and of all the beings of this world;
you have created the light of your saints,
the bright cloud of witnesses around us.
May our souls be your lamps, kindled and illumined by you.
May they shine and burn with your truth,
and never go out in darkness and ashes.
May we be your dwelling, shining from you, shining in you;
may we shine and our light never fail;
may we worship you always.
May we be kindled brightly and never extinguished.
Being filled with Christ's splendor,
may we shine within, so that the gloom of sin is cleared away,
and the light of everlasting life abides within us. *Amen.*

Forms for Prayers of the People for the Burial Rite

A.

Let us pray to God our Creator saying, Holy One, hear us (*or* Lord, have mercy).

Loving God, you have called your people together in the mystical body of Jesus Christ our Savior. Give to your whole Church in heaven and on earth your light and your peace.
Holy One, hear us.

Grant that all who have been baptized into Christ's death and resurrection may die daily to sin and rise to newness of life, and that we, with our Redeemer, may pass through the grave and gate of death to our joyful resurrection.
Holy One, hear us.

Grant to us who are still on our earthly pilgrimage, and who walk as yet by faith, that your Spirit may lead us in holiness and righteousness all our days.
Holy One, hear us.

Grant to your faithful people pardon and peace, that we may be cleansed from all our sin and serve you with a quiet mind.
Holy One, hear us.

Grant that N., increasing in the knowledge and love of you, may go from strength to strength in a new life of perfect service.
Holy One, hear us.

Grant to [N., N., *and*] all who mourn, a sure confidence in your tender mercy, that, casting all their sorrow on you, they may know the consolation of your love.
Holy One, hear us.

Give courage to all who are bereaved, that in the days ahead they may hold fast to the comfort of a holy hope, and joyful expectation of eternal life with those they love.
Holy One, hear us.

Help us entrust N. to your never-failing care and love. Receive *her* into the arms of your mercy, and remember *her* according to the favor you bear for your people.
Holy One, hear us.

Silence may be kept.

The Officiant concludes with one of the prayers on pp. 70-78.

B.

For N. *[our sister]*, let us pray to our Savior Jesus Christ who said: "I am Resurrection and I am Life."
Hear us, O Christ.

Jesus, you consoled Martha and Mary in their distress; be with us and all who mourn for N., and dry the tears of those who weep.
Hear us, O Christ.

Jesus, you wept at the grave of Lazarus, your friend. Comfort us in our sorrow.
Hear us, O Christ.

Jesus, you raised the dead to life. Give to [*our sister*] N. eternal life.
Hear us, O Christ.

Jesus, you promised paradise to the thief who repented. Bring
[*our sister*] N. to the joys of heaven.
Hear us, O Christ.

N. was washed in the waters of Baptism and anointed with the
Holy Spirit; give *her* a place in the company of your saints.
Hear us, O Christ.

N. was nourished with your Body and Blood in the Eucharist;
grant *her* a place at the table at the banquet you have promised
to your people at the close of the age.
Hear us, O Christ.

Comfort us in our sorrow at the death of N.; let our faith be our
consolation, and eternal life our hope.
Hear us, O Christ.

Silence may be kept.

The Officiant concludes with one of the prayers on pp. 70-78.

C.

Kaddish

*This is especially appropriate in some services, or at the Committal, where
members of the family or congregation are Jewish. It may be led by an appointed
member of the family.*

Magnified and sanctified be the great name of God in the world
that the Holy One created.
Blessed be God for ever.

May God establish the Kingdom in your life and in your days,
and in the lifetime of all people; quickly and speedily may it come;
and let us say Amen!
Blessed be God for ever.

Blessed, praised, and glorified, exalted, extolled, and honored, magnified and lauded be the name of the Holy One.
Blessed be God for ever.

Though God be high above all blessings and hymns, praises and consolations which are uttered in the world.
Blessed be God for ever.

May there be abundant peace from heaven and life for us and for all people, and let us say Amen!
Blessed be God for ever.

D.

God, your will for us is abundant life; receive N. now into the fullness of life in your presence.
Hear our prayer.

You know the thoughts of our hearts and our search for faith; shed the brightness of your light on N., who also sought understanding.
Hear our prayer.

You are greater than all our ideas and images of you; draw N. into the mystery of your being.
Hear our prayer.

We know you as perfect Mercy and Love; welcome N. in the grace of that love and mercy.
Hear our prayer.

We praise you as the giver of life; gather all who mourn into the hope of renewed life.
Hear our prayer.

The Church commends all who die to the care of Christ, the love of God, and the communion of the Holy Spirit; and so we commend N. to you, giving thanks for the gift of *her* life.
Hear our prayer.

Officiant

May the Holy One, to whom all the desires of our hearts are known before we ask, hear our prayers for N., and for all who mourn, and grant us newness of life, and peace. *Amen.*

Prayers for the Committal
of a Body at a Crematory

The Officiant may address the congregation, acknowledging briefly the purpose of their gathering, and bidding their prayers for the deceased and the bereaved.

Readings

Hear the words of Scripture to those who mourn:

Because of the Lord's great love, we are not consumed, for God's compassions never fail. They are new every morning. Great is your faithfulness! I say to myself, "The Lord is your portion; therefore I will wait for God." The Lord is good to those whose hope is in God, to the one who seeks God. It is good to wait quietly for the salvation of the Lord. *Lamentations 3:22 ff*

The souls of the righteous ones are in the hand of God, and no torment will ever touch them. In the eyes of those without under-standing they seem to have died, and their departure was thought to be mistreatment, and their going from us a violent fracture; but they are at peace. For though in the sight of others they were chas-tised; their hope is full of immortality. Having been corrected a little, they will receive great good, because God tested them and found them worthy of Godself; like gold in a crucible, God tried them, and like a sacrificial burnt offering accepted them. In the time of their examination, they will shine brightly, and will run like sparks through the field of stubble...the faithful will abide with God in love. *Wisdom 3:1-7, 9b Septuagint trans. J. M. Phillips*

Any of the readings from the burial office may be used in addition to or instead of the above.

Let us pray.

Eternal God, in whose love nothing is lost: Into your hands we commit your servant *N.*, whom you have known from before *she* was born and held in your watchful care. As *her* body is changed back to the energies and elements of the earth from which it came, may *she* return to you to be clothed in a shining resurrection body and joined in the joyful company of all the saints in light. Bless us who hold *her* in memory and cherish the good love and labor of *her* life. When morning comes, turn our separation into reunion and transform our grieving into joy, through Jesus Christ our Redeemer and your Holy Spirit who is breath and fire of love, who dwell with you, one God, now and for ever. *Amen.*

As the fire is lit, and the body is committed to the fire, silence is kept.
Then the following is said

We have entrusted *N.* to God's mercy,
and now in preparation for burial,
we give *her* body to the fire,
We look for the fullness of the resurrection
when Christ shall gather all the saints
to reign in glory. *Amen.*

People

Into your hands we commend *her* spirit,
for you have redeemed *her*, O Lord, O God of truth.
Keep *her* as the apple of your eye.
Hide *her* under the shadow of your wings.
Lord, have mercy;
Christ have mercy;
Lord have mercy.

Then the Officiant may say one or more of these anthems

Into paradise may the angels lead you.
At your coming, may the martyrs receive you,
and bring you into the holy city Jerusalem.

Lord, you now have set your servant free*
to go in peace as you have promised;
For these eyes of mine have seen the Savior,*
Whom you have prepared for all the world to see:
A light to enlighten the nations,*
and the glory of your people Israel.

The Spirit and the bride say "Come." And let everyone who hears
say, "Come." And let everyone who is thirsty come. Let anyone
who wishes take the water of life as a gift. The ransomed of the
Lord shall return, and come to Zion with singing; everlasting joy
shall be upon their heads; they shall obtain joy and gladness, and
sorrow and sighing shall flee away.   *Isaiah 35:10*

My heart is glad and my spirit rejoices; my body also rests secure.
For you do not give me up to Sheol, or let your faithful one see
the Pit. You show me the path of life and in your presence there
is fullness of joy; in your right hand are pleasures for evermore.
Psalm 16:9-11

The service concludes as follows:

People

In you, God our Hope,
life is changed, not ended.
To you we entrust our beloved one, N.
Receive *her* into your arms of mercy.
May *she* dwell in your presence for ever
and rejoice to see you face to face.

Officiant   Go in peace, putting your trust in God. Alleluia.
People   Thanks be to God. Alleluia.

A Service of Remembrance

For the forty-day or yearly commemoration of a death, the following rite is adapted from the Orthodox service, and is traditionally used at home. It may be used in church at the conclusion of the Eucharist or the Daily Office.

Officiant   Blessed is our God, always, now and for ever and to the ages of ages.

People   Amen.

The Trisagion is sung or said three times. (The Hymnal 1982, S102)

Holy God,
Holy and Mighty,
Holy Immortal One,
Have mercy upon us.

Officiant and People

God of Grace, we pray to you for *N.*, whom we love and see no longer. Grant to *her* eternal rest. Let light perpetual shine upon *her*. May *her* soul and souls of all the departed, through the mercy of God, rest in peace. *Amen.*

The anthem, "Give Rest, O Christ" is sung or said. (The Hymnal 1982, 355)

Give rest, O Christ, to your servant(s) with your saints,
where sorrow and pain are no more,
neither sighing, but life everlasting.

You only are immortal, the creator and maker of mankind; and we are mortal, formed of the earth, and to earth shall we return. For so did you ordain when you created me, saying, "You are dust, and to dust you shall return." All of us go down to the dust; yet even at the grave we make our song: Alleluia, alleluia, alleluia.

Give rest, O Christ, to your servant(s) with your saints,
where sorrow and pain are no more,
neither sighing, but life everlasting.

Officiant	The Lord be with you.
People	And also with you.
Officiant	Let us pray.

O God of the living and the dead, you have trampled upon death and abolished the power of evil, giving life to your world. Give to your departed servant N. rest in a place of light, in a place of tranquility, in a place of refreshment, where there is no pain, nor sorrow, nor suffering. For you, Christ our God, are the resurrection, the life, and the repose of your servant N., and to you we give glory, with your eternal Father and your all-holy, good, and life-giving Spirit, now and for ever. *Amen.*

Officiant

May Christ, who rose from the dead and has authority over the living and the dead, have mercy on us and save us. May the prayers of the Blessed Virgin Mary, and all the saints in glory, strengthen us all and welcome N. in the heavenly places. *Amen.*

Anthem	Christ is risen from the dead, trampling down death by death and giving life to those in the tomb.

Suggested Songs for Burial Rites

Hymn	Tune/Lyricist/Composer	Source
Amazing Grace	*New Britain*	*LEVAS II - 181*
Be Still My Soul	*Finlandia,* Jean Sibelius	*Lead Me, Guide Me - 163*
Blessed Assurance	Fanny J. Crosby & Pheobe	P. Knapp *LEVAS II - 184*
Breathe on me, Breath of God	*Nova Vita*	*The Hymnal 1982 - 508*
Christ the Victorious	*Russia,* Alexis Lvov	*The Hymnal 1982 - 358*
Come and Go to that Land	Spiritual, arr. Pamela Warrick Smith	GIA Publications
Come to Me	Spiritual, arr. R. Nathaniel Dett	*LEVAS II - 156*
Deep River	Spiritual *LEVAS II - 8*	
For All the Saints	*Sine Nomine* Ralph Vaughn Williams	*The Hymnal 1982 - 287*
God be in my Head	*Lytlington,* Sydney Hugo Nicholson	*The Hymnal 1982 - 694*
Going up Yonder	Walter Hawkins	*Songs of Zion - 181*
Guide Me, O My Great Redeemer	*Zion*	*The New Century Hymnal - 19*
His Eye is on the Sparrow	Civilla Martin & Charles H. Gabriel	*LEVAS II - 191*
I'll Fly Away	Albert Brumley	*Lead Me, Guide Me - 149*
If I Can Help Somebody	Alma B. Androzzo	
It is Well with my Soul	Haratio Spafford & Philip P. Bliss	*LEVAS II - 188*
It's a Highway to Heaven	Mary Gardner & Thomas A. Dorsey	*African American Heritage Hymn*
Just a Closer Walk with Thee	American Folk Song	*LEVAS II - 72*
Kum Bah Yah	Spiritual	*LEVAS II - 162*
The Last Mile of the Way	Johnson Oatman, Jr., William Edie Marks	*New National Baptist Hymnal - 235*

May choirs of angels lead you	*Christus, der ist mein Leben*	*The Hymnal 1982 - 356*
My Heavenly Father Watches Over Me	Charles H. Gabriel	*LEVAS II - 59*
O Father, on your Love we call	*Melita*	Jean Holloway, lyrics Unknown
On Jordan's Stormy Banks I Stand	American Melody	*LEVAS II -9*
Only a Look	Anna Shepherd	*Songs of Zion - 197*
Only What You Do for Christ Will Last	Raymond Rasberry	*Lead Me, Guide Me - 286*
Over My Head	Spiritual	*Songs of Zion - 167*
Shine on Me	Spiritual	*Lead Me, Guide Me - 160*
Soon and Very Soon	Andrae Crouch	*LEVAS II - 14*
Soon-a Will Be Done	Spiritual	*Songs of Zion - 158*
Steal Away	Spiritual	*LEVAS II - 103*
There's a Wideness in God's Mercy	*St. Helena* Calvin Hampton	*Hymnal 1982 - 469*
Want to Go to Heaven When I Die	Spiritual	*Lead me Guide me - 315*
We Shall Behold Him	Dotty Rambo	*African American Hymnal - 583*
We'll Understand It Better By and By	Charles A. Tindley	*LEVAS II - 207*
We're Marching to Zion	Isaac Watts / Robert S. Lowry	*LEVAS II - 12*
When We All Get to Heaven	Eliza Hewitt & Emily Wilson	*LEVAS II – 20*

Notes for Burial Rites

Introduction (p. 1) Modeled on lengthier introductions to be found in the *Alternative Services Book* (1980), the *Book of Alternative Services* (1985), and *Common Worship* (2000), this piece illustrates the ritual process that has become customary in the Church's burial rites. It also provides a short "teaching piece" for congregations that wish to reproduce something about the nature of the service in parish funeral bulletins.

Outline of the Rites (p. 3) This provides a practical companion to the Introduction. It traces the ritual process noted there, listing useful sequences and options. It was inspired by the schematic included in an early version of the Evangelical Lutheran Church in America's *Renewing Worship* (2005).

Prayers for a Vigil (p. 13) The first alternative augments the form of the rite found in BCP 1979, p. 465. The second comes from the Church of St. John the Evangelist, Boston, with antiphons from the *Proper of the Seasons* of the Society of St. Margaret.

Reception of the Body (p. 21) The first alternative is a redaction of the rite found in BCP 1979, p. 466. The second alternative is a slight revision of the rite found in *Common Worship*. The third alternative is taken from *Renewing Worship*.

The Burial of the Dead (p. 27)

Anthems (p. 27) The first set of anthems are from the BCP 1979, p. 491, with quotations from the Revised Standard Version of the Bible replaced by material from the New Revised Standard Version. The second set of anthems is based on material in *Common*

Worship. The third set has been revised from the BCP 1979, p. 492.

The optional introductory sentence comes from *Common Worship.*

Collects (p. 29)
1. A revision of collect #2, BCP 1979, p. 493
2. From *Burial Services,* 1987, the Episcopal Church of Scotland
3. From the *Book of Alternative Services*
4. From *Common Worship*
5. An original composition
6. From *Renewing Worship*

Lectionary (p. 32) The entire lectionary from BCP 1979 is retained, with additions from the *Alternative Service Book* and the *Book of Alternative Services.* These additions offer the congregation and the preacher texts that address pastoral situations not necessarily covered in the BCP lectionary. The familiar readings from Romans and 1 Corinthians suggest useful cuts that make those readings more compact.

Proper prefaces (p. 34) The two additional proper prefaces are original compositions.

Postcommunion prayer (p. 34) This is a revision of the BCP text.

The Commendation (p. 35) The substitution of the first person plural in the *Kontokian* follows a suggestion by Marion Hatchett. The prayer "God our creator…" comes from *Common Worship.* The alternative final prayer for use when the Committal does not follow immediately is the concluding prayer from the BCP Good Friday Rite.

The Committal: (p. 59) The new alternative prayer "We have entrusted…" comes from *Common Worship,* while "Holy God…" comes from *Renewing Worship.* The optional litany, p. 61, is from *Renewing Worship.*

Committal under Special Circumstances: (p. 62) This provides for situations not covered by the texts in BCP 1979, including the transfer of bodies from a major burial rite held in one place to a committal held elsewhere, as well as the reality that there are a growing number of cemeteries that do not permit graveside rites. The new alternative committal prayers come from *Renewing Worship.*

Consecration of a Grave: (p. 65) The first alternative is from *Renewing Worship.* The second is adapted from BCP 1979. The third comes from *Common Worship.*

Burial of one who does not profess the Christian Faith (p. 66) Sometimes, there are pastoral reasons for a burial office that acknowledges a non-believing member of an otherwise churched family. In the case of an interfaith marriage, the deceased may have family and friends who continue to embrace another tradition, although he or she attended church with his or her spouse. The design of the rite follows the pattern in Bernardin's *Burial Services,* although most of the prayers are original.

Additional Prayers:
#1 through #9 (pp. 70-71) These are revisions of material from BCP, 1979.
#10 (p. 72) From *A New Zealand Prayer Book,* Collins, 1989
#11 (p. 72) From *Burial Services,* 1987, The Episcopal Church of Scotland
#12 (p. 72) From *Burial Services,* 1987, The Episcopal Church of Scotland
#13 (p. 72) From the Greek Orthodox Burial Service
#14 (p. 73) From *Burial Services,* The Episcopal Church of Scotland
#15 (p. 73) From *Celebrating Common Prayer,* Mowbray's, 1992
#16 (p. 73) From *Celebrating Common Prayer,* Mowbray's, 1992
#17 (p. 74) An original composition
#18 (p. 74) An original composition
#19 (p. 75) An original composition

#20 (p. 75) Adapted from BCP, 1979
#21 (p. 75) An original composition
#22 (p. 76) An original composition
#23 (p. 76) An original composition
#24 (p. 77) An original composition
#25 (p. 77) An original composition
#26 (p. 78) A prayer of St. Anselm – see *Enriching Our Worship 2*,
 p. 57, and note on p. 148.
#27 (p. 78) From the Mozarabic tradition

Prayers for a Committal of a body at a Crematory (p. 84)
Readings (p. 84) The version of Lamentations 3:22 and Wisdom
3:1-7, 9B represent an original translation by the Rev. Dr. J. M.
Phillips.

Prayers "Eternal God..." (p. 85) and "We have entrusted..." (p. 85)
are original compositions. "In you, God our hope..." (p. 86) is an
original composition.

A Service of Remembrance (p. 87) As noted in the introductory
rubric, this is adapted from the Orthodox tradition – an original
composition.

www.ingramcontent.com/pod-product-compliance
Lightning Source LLC
Jackson TN
JSHW080853211224
75817JS00002B/26